¡Nuestra maravillosa Tierra! / Our Exciting Earth

ARRECIFES
REEFS

Tanner Billing
Traducido por / Translated by Diana Osorio

Please visit our website, www.garethstevens.com.
For a free color catalog of all our high-quality books, call toll free 1-800-542-2595 or fax 1-877-542-2596.

Library of Congress Cataloging-in-Publication Data
Names: Billings, Tanner, author.
Title: Arrecifes / Reefs / Tanner Billings.
Description: New York : Gareth Stevens Publishing, [2023] | Series: ¡Nuestra maravillosa Tierra! / Our Exciting Earth | Includes index.
Identifiers: LCCN 2021039095 | ISBN 9781538276136 (Library Binding) | ISBN 9781538276143 (eBook)
Subjects: LCSH: Reefs–Juvenile literature. | Coral reefs and islands–Juvenile literature. | Reef plants–Juvenile literature. | Reef organisms–Juvenile literature.
Classification: LCC GB461 .B55 2023 | DDC 577.7/89–dc23/eng/20211008
LC record available at https://lccn.loc.gov/2021039095

First Edition

Published in 2023 by
Gareth Stevens Publishing
29 East 21st Street
New York, NY 10010

Copyright © 2023 Gareth Stevens Publishing

Translator: Diana Osorio
Editor, Spanish: Diana Osorio
Editor, English: Kate Mikoley
Designer: Tanya Dellaccio

Photo credits: Cover V_E/Shutterstock.com; p. 5 silvae/Shutterstock.com; p. 7 Damsea/Shutterstock.com; p. 9 Dobermaraner/Shutterstock.com; p. 11 SARAWUT KUNDEJ/Shutterstock.com; p. 13 Pawe? Borówka/Shutterstock.com; pp. 15, 19 Volodymyr Goinyk/Shutterstock.com; p. 17 stephan kerkhofs/Shutterstock.com; p. 21 tororo reaction/Shutterstock.com; p. 23 ChameleonsEye/Shutterstock.com.

All rights reserved. No part of this book may be reproduced in any form without permission in writing from the publisher, except by a reviewer.

Printed in the United States of America

CPSIA compliance information: Batch #CSGS23: For further information contact Gareth Stevens, New York, New York at 1-800-542-2595.

Contenido

¿Qué es un arrecife?............ 4
Qué geniales son los corales........ 8
Coral colorido............. 14
Grandes arrecifes........... 18
Palabras que debes aprender..... 24
Índice................ 24

Contents

What's a Reef?............. 4
Cool Coral............... 8
Colorful Coral............ 14
Great Big Reefs........... 18
Words to Know............ 24
Index................. 24

Un arrecife se encuentra en el mar. Está cerca de la cumbre.

....

A reef is in the sea.
It is near the top.

Algunos son de roca.

....

Some are made of rock.

Algunos están hechos de pequeños animales. Estos animales son corales.

....

Some are made of tiny animals. These are coral.

El coral tiene
una parte sólida.
Puede formar
un arrecife.

....

Coral has a hard part.
It can form a reef.

Aquí viven
muchos peces.
Las plantas
también lo hacen.

....

Lots of fish live here.
Plants do too.

Los corales son de muchos colores.

....

Corals are many colors.

Algunos son rojos.
Otros son azules.

....

Some are red.
Some are blue.

Los arrecifes crecen durante muchos años.

....

Reefs grow for many years.

Pueden ser grandes.
La Gran Barrera de
Coral es grande.

······························

They can be big.
The Great Barrier
Reef is big.

Puedes ir a un arrecife.
¡No toques nada!

....

You can go to a reef.
Don't touch!

Palabras que debes aprender
Words to Know

coral/
coral

pez/
fish

planta/
plant

Índice / Index

coral / coral, 8, 10, 14

pez / fish, 12

rocas / rock, 6